Baseball Legends

Hank Aaron
Grover Cleveland Alexander
Ernie Banks
Johnny Bench
Yogi Berra
Roy Campanella
Roberto Clemente
Ty Cobb
Dizzy Dean
Joe DiMaggio
Bob Feller
Jimmie Foxx
Lou Gehrig
Bob Gibson
Rogers Hornsby
Walter Johnson
Sandy Koufax
Mickey Mantle
Christy Mathewson
Willie Mays
Stan Musial
Satchel Paige
Brooks Robinson
Frank Robinson
Jackie Robinson
Babe Ruth
Duke Snider
Warren Spahn
Willie Stargell
Honus Wagner
Ted Williams
Carl Yastrzemski
Cy Young

CHELSEA HOUSE PUBLISHERS

NEW

BASEBALL LEGENDS

MICKEY MANTLE

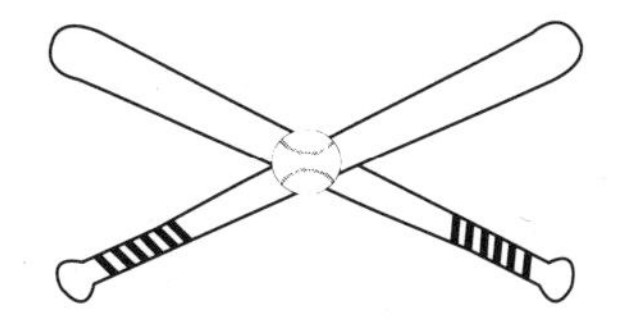

Mark Gallagher
and
Neil Gallagher

Introduction by
Jim Murray

Senior Consultant
Earl Weaver

CHELSEA HOUSE PUBLISHERS
New York • Philadelphia

Produced by James Charlton Associates
New York, New York.

Designed by Hudson Studio
Ossining, New York.

Typesetting by LinoGraphics
New York, New York.

Picture research by Carolann Hawkins
Cover illustration by Dan O'Leary

Copyright © 1991 by Chelsea House Publishers, a division of Main Line Book Co. All rights reserved. Printed and bound in the United States of America.

3 5 7 9 8 6 4

Library of Congress Cataloging-in-Publication Data

Gallagher, Mark.
Mickey Mantle / Mark Gallagher and Neil Gallagher ; introd. by Jim Murray.
p. cm. — (Baseball legends)
Includes bibliographical references and index.
Summary: A biography of the New York Yankee famed for his legendary hitting ability.
ISBN 0-7910-1181-X — ISBN 0-7910-1215-8 (pbk.)
1. Mantle, Mickey, 1931- —Juvenile literature. 3. New York Yankees (Baseball team)—Juvenile literature. [1. Mantle, Mickey, 1931- . 2. Baseball players.] I. Gallagher, Neil, 1941-
II. Title. III. Series.
GV865.M24G35 1991
796.357'092—dc20 90-46664
[92] CIP
[B] AC

921
Man

CONTENTS

156505

WHAT MAKES A STAR

Jim Murray

No one has ever been able to explain to me the mysterious alchemy that makes one man a .350 hitter and another player, more or less identical in physical makeup, hard put to hit .200. You look at an Al Kaline, who played with the Detroit Tigers from 1953 to 1974. He was pale, stringy, almost poetic-looking. He always seemed to be struggling against a bad case of mononucleosis. But with a bat in his hands, he was King Kong. During his career, he hit 399 home runs, rapped out 3,007 hits, and compiled a .297 batting average.

Form isn't the reason. The first time anybody saw Roberto Clemente step into the batter's box for the Pittsburgh Pirates, the best guess was that Clemente would be back in Double A ball in a week. He had one foot in the bucket and held his bat at an awkward angle—he looked as though he couldn't hit an outside pitch. A lot of other ballplayers may have had a better-looking stance. Yet they never led the National League in hitting in four different years, the way Clemente did.

Not every ballplayer is born with the ability to hit a curveball. Nor is exceptional hand-eye coordination the key to heavy hitting. Big-league locker rooms are filled with players who have all the attributes, save one: discipline. Every baseball man can tell you a story about a pitcher who throws a ball faster than anyone has ever seen but who has no control on or *off* the field.

The Hall of Fame is full of people who transformed themselves into great ballplayers by working at the sport, by studying the game, and making sacrifices. They're overachievers—and winners. If you want to find them, just watch the World Series. Or simply read about New York Yankee great Lou Gehrig; Ted Williams, "the Splendid Splinter" of the Boston Red Sox; or the Dodgers' strikeout king Sandy Koufax.

A pitcher *should* be able to win a lot of ballgames with a 98-miles-per-hour fastball. But what about the pitcher who wins 20 games a year with a fastball so slow that you can catch it with your teeth? Bob Feller of the Cleveland Indians got into the Hall of Fame with a blazing fastball that glowed in the dark. National League star Grover Cleveland Alexander got there with a pitch that took considerably longer to reach the plate; but when it did arrive, the pitch was exactly where Alexander wanted it to be—and the last place the batter expected it to be.

There are probably more players with exceptional ability who didn't make it to the major leagues than there are who did. A number of great hitters, bored with fielding practice, had to be dropped from their team because their home-run production didn't make up for their lapses in the field. And then there are players like Brooks Robinson of the Baltimore Orioles, who made himself into a human vacuum cleaner at third base because he knew that working hard to become an expert fielder would win him a job in the big leagues.

A star is not something that flashes through the sky. That's a comet. Or a meteor. A star is something you can steer ships by. It stays in place and gives off a steady glow; it is fixed, permanent. A star works at being a star.

And that's how you tell a star in baseball. He shows up night after night and takes pride in how brightly he shines. He's Willie Mays running so hard his hat keeps falling off; Ty Cobb sliding to stretch a single into a double; Lou Gehrig, after being fooled in his first two at-bats, belting the next pitch off the light tower because he's taken the time to study the pitcher. Stars never take themselves for granted. That's why they're stars.

1 THE PINCH-HIT HOME RUN

Mickey Mantle, star centerfielder of the New York Yankees, was chasing after a long fly ball and another great major league season when he crashed into a chain-link fence in Baltimore's Memorial Stadium. The three-time American League Most Valuable Player lay at the bottom of the fence, a bone in his left foot broken and parts of his left knee damaged. The ball had just cleared the fence, and the Orioles' Brooks Robinson was trotting home.

It was June 5th, and Mickey Mantle's 1963 season was at its peak. He had doubled, singled, and walked in the game, and so all-out was his pursuit of Robinson's drive that he ran full-speed into the fence, his spikes entangling in the barrier's curled wire strands. Mantle's teammates gathered around him, then carried him off the field.

Doctors placed Mantle's foot in a cast and

Following his injury on June 5, 1963, Mantle needs to be helped off a chartered airplane at New York's LaGuardia Airport.

announced that he would probably be out of action for the rest of the season. Then they handed him some crutches and asked if he knew how to use them. "I've lived with them," he answered flatly. The injuries, while serious in themselves, were just the latest in a long and discouraging string of physical setbacks endured by Mickey Mantle.

Would the battered centerfielder have the will to come back once more? Or would he throw in the towel? Previously, he had been able to recover during the off-season. This time, however, he would be forced to watch the Yankees take the field without him, game after game—61 more of them.

It was rumored that the 31-year-old Mantle would retire. Indeed, thoughts of quitting baseball crossed his mind. As the season dragged on, his spirits sank deeper.

Yankee manager Ralph Houk asked Mantle to travel with the team. Houk said that the Yankees needed Mantle's leadership, but almost certainly the manager sensed it was the injured star who needed a boost of morale. But Mantle was restless on the bench and grew weary of dealing with the constant "When will you play?" questions from reporters and fans.

On August 4th, two months after being injured, Mantle watched from the dugout as Baltimore beat the Yankees in the first game of a Sunday doubleheader at Yankee Stadium. In the second game, he felt a stirring of excitement as the Orioles took a 10–9 lead into the seventh inning. He was not yet fully recovered, but he knew he could be called on to pinch-hit. He had told Houk he was ready to bat and promised that he would not risk reinjuring himself by running out a grounder.

Mickey Mantle and Joe DiMaggio, two Yankee legends. Mantle played alongside DiMaggio in the outfield in 1951, and then took over center field the next season when DiMaggio retired.

With Yankee pitcher Steve Hamilton due up in the bottom of the inning, a pinch-hit situation was clearly taking shape. Mantle wandered over to the bat rack. As soon as the fans on the third-base side—opposite the Yankee dugout—spotted his movements, they began to clap. Soon, almost all of the 38,555 spectators were cheering in anticipation of Mantle's appearance. And when he stepped out of the dugout, bat in hand, the crowd rose as one in a thunderous ovation.

Mantle walked stiff-legged to the plate. "I was so nervous about the ovation I got when I went to the plate that my hands were trembling," he recalled. Goose bumps rose on his arms as he stepped into the right-handed batter's box to face left-handed pitcher George Brunet.

Mantle did not want to let the fans down. He said later he would have been satisfied just to make solid contact and hit a single. But after

The Yankees lost the first game of an August 4, 1963, doubleheader against the Orioles, and were losing the second, 10–9, when Mantle returned to the lineup in the 7th inning as a pinch-hitter. He took a strike and then lined a homer to tie the game. The Yankees eventually won, 11–10.

taking one strike, Mantle swung at a fastball and drove it skyward. Oriole left fielder Jackie Brandt raced to the fence and tried to make the catch, but the ball skimmed over the barrier for a home run. Another deafening roar filled Yankee Stadium.

Mantle had not believed his drive would reach the seats. He was hobbling as quickly as he could toward first base when he saw the umpire signal a home run. "I'm a lucky stiff," he told himself. "Gee, but I'm a lucky stiff." He crossed the plate and was greeted with an outpouring of congratulations in the dugout. His teammates were flushed, exuberant; he, in contrast, was pale, chilled, shaken. How had it felt to circle the bases again? someone wanted to know. "I don't remember running," Mantle replied. "It's a long trip, and it's the first time I've made that trip in a long time."

Years later, Mantle was asked to pick his 10 greatest baseball memories for an article by Joe Donnelly in *Sport* magazine. Not surprisingly, that comeback round-tripper was among them. "If I had to pick one as the greatest of all out of the ten memories," Mantle said, "this might be it."

The pinch-hit homer was part of Mantle's career-long pattern of overcoming adversity. That he considered himself lucky in hitting the home run, that he wanted so badly to come through for the fans, say something about Mickey Mantle. The moment itself may have been a bit lucky for him—the ball barely cleared the fence—but "lucky" is not an appropriate word for a ballplayer who excelled so consistently in the face of hounding injuries. "Great" is a much better way to describe Mickey Mantle.

MIAMI

2

THE UNLUCKY LUCKY STIFF

Mickey Charles Mantle was born on October 20, 1931, in Spavinaw, Oklahoma. He was the oldest child of Lovell and Elvin "Mutt" Mantle. He had twin brothers, Roy and Ray, and a sister, Susie. A true baseball fan, Mutt named his first son after catcher Mickey Cochrane. And almost as soon as little Mickey could walk, Mutt had him swinging a bat at tennis balls.

Mutt, a left-hander, would also have his own father, Grandpa Charley, pitch. Mickey soon learned that he had to bat lefty when the right-handed Charley was throwing. It felt like being asked to drink while upside-down, but the boy was eager to please his father. Mickey not only made his dad happy, he made himself a switch-hitter—as time would prove, baseball's greatest ever.

To Mutt, baseball was not only a glorious game but a welcome break from the ore mines of northeastern Oklahoma, where he worked long, hard hours underground. His one brief attempt at farming, at making a living in the fresh air and

Mickey, 14, in the uniform of the Miami, Oklahoma, team.

sunshine, was as cursed as the 1930s, when the Great Depression took hold of America. A period of great economic hardship, the Depression weighed heavily on Oklahoma, and many Oklahomans left for California and other places in search of jobs. But the Mantles stayed. They were a tightly knit family with a love of fun and sports. Baseball was more than just a game to Mutt. It was his one hope for a better life for his oldest son.

Growing up in Commerce, Oklahoma, 50 miles away from Spavinaw, Mickey played baseball, basketball, and was a high-school football star. As far as Mutt Mantle was concerned, football caused a lot of injuries and could jeopardize a baseball career. In Oklahoma, however, football is king, and so Mutt tried to put aside his fears and cheer the exploits of his speedy, hard-running son.

One day, however, Mickey bruised his shin during a practice scrimmage. The shin swelled up overnight and turned black and blue. Doctors diagnosed it as a flare-up of osteomyelitis, a bone disease. Mickey's leg was so severely afflicted, a doctor informed Mickey's mother, it might have to be amputated. "The hell it will!" was Lovell Mantle's response. Fortunately, Mickey received numerous injections of a recently discovered drug, penicillin, at Crippled Children's Hospital in Oklahoma City, and the leg quickly improved. He was discharged with his first set of crutches and firm advice to take it easy.

Mickey did take it easy as best he could. In time, he tried a little basketball and then some baseball. Then more and more baseball. He was playing for the Whiz Kids, an amateur team in nearby Baxter Springs, Kansas, when New York

In 1950, Mantle was the shortstop for the Yankees' minor-league team in Joplin, Missouri. He led the Western League in hitting with a .383 average, but also led in errors with 55.

Yankee scout Tim Greenwade signed him. While Baxter Springs was the "territory" of St. Louis's two major league teams, the Cardinals and the Browns, the Browns had shown little interest in Mickey, and the Cardinals were slow to make an offer, possibly because Mickey was still somewhat short and slight. But Greenwade saw the bright star in Mantle. From the beginning, Greenwade experienced a sensation he said was akin to what Yankee scout Paul Krichell must have felt when he first laid eyes on Lou Gehrig and phoned the Yankees to say he had "found another Babe Ruth."

Mickey spent two years in the minors, primarily at shortstop. Then, in 1951, he attended the club's Phoenix, Arizona, instructional school, which preceded spring training.

The Yankees had several outstanding prospects, but Mantle was the most impressive of all.

Because they were hoping he could take over Joe DiMaggio's center-field spot in a few years, manager Casey Stengel and his staff overlooked Mantle's ragged fielding at shortstop. Instead, they focused on his power and his speed. Stengel could hardly believe his stopwatch: It took the youngster just over 3 seconds to reach first base, and he could round all 4 bases in under 13.

Mickey, who had played for the Class C Joplin, Missouri, Miners the previous season, was picked to work out with the big club during spring training. A feature of the spring camp was a tour of California. Mickey looked good all along the tour route, but his showing at the University of Southern California (USC) was especially impressive.

His four hits there included a triple and two gargantuan homers, one from each side of the plate. The left-handed shot "was like it wasn't real," USC coach Rod Dedeaux raved. By many accounts, the ball traveled more than 600 feet. USC students mobbed Mantle after the game. Less than two years earlier, Mickey had been playing in the sandlots of Oklahoma. Now, he was handing out autographs under the California sun.

And yet Stengel still had to persuade general manager George Weiss to let Mickey start in right field for the world-famous Yankees. Weiss leaned toward giving the youngster a little more seasoning before subjecting him to the pressures of major league ball. When Stengel finally convinced Weiss to take the rookie back to New York for the regular season, the colorful manager explained his reasoning this way: His prize 19 year old was indeed "a green pea" who might miss some fly balls. "On the other hand," he added, “he’ll hit some nobody’s going to catch.”

New York fans had been reading about Mickey’s achievements all spring and could hardly wait to see the young star. But there was no way Mickey could live up to his spring-training batting average of .402, built in part against college kids and prospects trying to make big-league teams. Veteran pitchers would often have their way with the inexperienced rookie. And while Mickey’s speed did make him better suited to the outfield than shortstop, his original position in professional baseball, he still had lots to learn at the plate. As the regular season got underway, he struggled to make contact. In a Memorial Day doubleheader, he fanned five times in a row.

At that point, Stengel sent Mickey down to the Yankees’ top farm club, the Kansas City Blues. When his slump continued there, Mickey came to a discouraging conclusion: If you can’t hit a baseball, he reasoned, you can’t play the game. So why bother? No sooner had he shared this sentiment with Mutt on the telephone than his dad was off to Kansas City. The two sat and talked for hours, and finally Mickey decided to give the game another try. Before long, he had lifted his average to .361, and by late August he was back in the majors.

Despite his early-season problems, Mantle hit .267 for New York while collecting 13 homers and 65 RBIs. His home run on September 19th, when New York was clinging to the league lead by only 3 percentage points, produced a key win in the club’s successful pennant drive.

Mutt, naturally, traveled to New York for the 1951 World Series with the New York Giants. The whole family could not afford the long trip, so Lovell Mantle remained in Oklahoma and rooted long-distance with her other children. In his autobiography *The Education of a Baseball Player*, Mickey called her a rabid fan and remembered how she would alter his uniforms to fit him perfectly, so that he would "look the part of a real ballplayer."

Mutt was in the Yankee dugout during the second game of the Series when his son caught his spikes in a drain cover while chasing a fly ball hit by Willie Mays. Mickey heard a sickening snap, and then he fell.

The next day, Mickey and Mutt took a taxi to New York's Lenox Hill Hospital. As they were getting out of the cab, Mickey leaned on his dad for support, and Mutt collapsed. Mickey had been worried about his father, who had lost so much weight he could hardly keep his pants up, but he had not realized how weak Mutt had become. The Lenox Hill doctors were also con-

Mantle and his bride-to-be, Merlyn Johnson, before an exhibition game in Kansas City in April 1951.

cerned about Mutt's condition, and so the two Mantles ended up sharing a room.

Mickey had ripped the ligaments around his right knee. As he was being treated, tests were run on Mutt. In the meantime, the two patients watched the rest of the Series on television. They cheered as the Yankees, down two games to one, came back to claim the world championship over their crosstown rivals, the New York Giants. But even as he savored his team's triumph, Mickey knew there was plenty wrong with his knee. Nobody had to tell him that. But what was wrong with Mutt?

Mickey, still a teenager, would soon get the answer from a grim-faced doctor. His dad had cancer and was dying.

After returning to Oklahoma with his father, Mickey bought a house for his parents with the World Series money he had earned. Then, two days before Christmas, he married Merlyn Johnson, a former high-school majorette from Picher, Oklahoma. The couple had met at a football game in 1949.

Mickey was so involved with family matters that he paid little attention to the December 1951 retirement of the Yankees' legendary centerfielder, Joe DiMaggio. But a gaping hole now beckoned in the middle of the Yankee outfield, and Casey Stengel was looking forward to filling it with the fleet-footed Mickey Mantle.

Mantle was still hobbling when he reported to spring camp in 1952, though, and he was unable to cover the vast center field. Instead, he was in the lineup, in right field, when the Yankees opened the season. But not for long. Within a few weeks, he was on his way home to Oklahoma for the funeral of the father he loved so dearly.

GREAT EXPECTATIONS

Mickey Mantle's boyhood was over. Boys cannot lead families, and Mickey was now leading two families—his dad's, with a widowed mother and three children still at home, and the family he and Merlyn were setting out to build.

Fortunately, his injured knee was getting stronger, and on May 20, 1952, Mantle returned to the lineup as the Yankees' centerfielder. Batting third, he rapped out two hits from each side of the plate.

Mantle kept on hitting, and he did the job defensively as well as offensively despite the pressure of being DiMaggio's successor. He finished the season batting .311, with 23 home runs and 87 RBIs—good enough for third place in the American League's Most Valuable Player voting.

The Yankees won the pennant and, in a grueling seven-game World Series, defeated the

Mantle, one of the fastest runners in baseball, beats out a bunt in game 1 of the 1952 World Series against the Dodgers. Gil Hodges takes the late throw as Jackie Robinson backs him up.

Brooklyn Dodgers. For Mickey, it was a magnificent Series. He hit .345 and broke a 2–2 tie in the deciding game with a home run, then drove in an insurance run as the Yankees triumphed, 4–2.

After the game, Dodger second baseman Jackie Robinson popped into the Yankee clubhouse to shake Mickey's hand. It was a classy gesture that Mantle, who was a notorious sore loser, admitted he could never make.

"Mantle beat us," Robinson said. "He was the difference between the two clubs. They didn't miss Joe DiMaggio. It was Mickey Mantle who killed us."

By 1953, at the age of 22, Mickey Mantle had become a successful big-league ballplayer, and he was making the most of his success. He had had his share of good times in the minors on *and* off the field, and he was looking forward to more of the same now that he was a member of the 1952 world champions.

Teammates Billy Martin and Whitey Ford were of similar mind and became his mirth-seeking companions—the "three amigos" they were sometimes called. On one occasion after a 1953 preseason game in Cincinnati, they became so absorbed in the pursuit of fun in nearby Covington, Kentucky, that they lost track of time and missed the team train. They figured they would simply fly to the site of the next game, Pittsburgh. However, when bad weather kept the planes on the ground, they learned a major league lesson: A two-state cab ride can cost $500.

To make matters worse, Stengel was not amused by their late arrival. Mantle was exhausted, but the manager made him play anyway. Tired as he was, Mickey still hit one of only three home runs ever to clear the 100-foot-high Forbes Field grandstand. "Nice hit, Mickey" was all Stengel said when he greeted him at the plate.

Mantle's 1953 stats dipped to .295 and 21 home runs, not bad for most players. But Mantle was not supposed to be like most players. He was supposed to be a superstar. His critics paid little attention to his injuries, however. All they saw was a bubblegum-blowing upstart who seemed unfit to fill the great DiMaggio's shoes.

Nevertheless, Mantle was establishing himself as one of the greatest longball hitters in baseball history. To some, including Stengel, that was part of his problem. They felt that maybe Mantle was getting carried away with swinging for the fences.

Eight days after his preseason blast at Forbes Field, Mantle had launched an incredible regular-season right-handed drive against the Wash-

On April 17, 1953, Mantle used a borrowed bat to hit the longest home run in the history of Washington's venerable Griffith Stadium, a clout of 565 feet that landed in a backyard. The bat and ball are now in the Hall of Fame.

ington Senators. The magnificence of this home run moved Arthur "Red" Patterson, the Yankees' publicity director, to try and determine its actual distance. Patterson, who retrieved the battered baseball outside the park, figured it had traveled 565 feet, and thus gave birth to the notion of the "tape measure" homer.

The "Washington wallop," as this blast became known, was hit on April 17, 1953, and was the first ever to clear the left-field bleachers in Griffith Stadium. It started baseball people talking for days and is still regarded as one of the longest home runs ever hit.

Mantle planted landmark homers around the league throughout the 1953 season. He hit one ball completely out of old Busch Stadium in St. Louis against the Browns. He cleared the roof at Philadelphia's Connie Mack Stadium and twice reached the right-field roof at Detroit's Tiger Stadium (then called Briggs Stadium).

But he saved his most impressive homer that year for Yankee Stadium. There, on September 12th, his right-handed shot was still upward bound as it banged into the seats high above left field. Yankee coach Bill Dickey, who began his playing career in 1928, had just finished saying that the legendary longballers of his era, Babe Ruth and Jimmie Foxx, had all hit balls harder than Mantle. As Mantle's home run disappeared into the upper deck, Dickey told his listeners, "Forget what I said." He had to admit that Mantle's was the hardest-hit shot he had ever seen.

Despite such dramatic moments, Mantle was still not playing up to expectations. Stengel wanted him to shorten his swing and concentrate on his batting average. The manager was as

In game 5 of the 1953 World Series, Mantle hits the 4th grand slam in World Series history to ice an 11–7 Yankee victory. Joe Collins (15), Hank Bauer (9), and Yogi Berra (8), all of whom scored on the hit, greet Mantle as Dodgers catcher Roy Campanella watches.

impressed as everyone else with the awesomeness of Mantle's drives. But he was looking for fewer strikeouts and more opportunities for the star slugger to reach base and be driven in by some of the Yankees' other heavy hitters.

Mantle did his part in the 1953 World Series as the Yankees beat the Dodgers for a record fifth-straight world championship. He stroked a two-run homer in game 2 and contributed a grand-slam home run to the Yanks' 11–7 victory in game 5. But it was his sidekick Billy Martin who did most of the good work for the Yankees, collecting a dozen hits, 2 of them homers, in 24 at-bats.

If the Yankees of 1953 looked invincible, the

1954 season would prove they were not. In historical terms, it was "the year the Yankees didn't win the pennant." Instead, they finished in second place behind the Cleveland Indians.

New York was again at the top of the American League as the 1955 season came to a close, and so was Mickey Mantle. That year he shed his role as teammate Yogi Berra's power twin, outhomering Berra, 37 to 27, to lead the league in that department. Yet it was Berra who was named the league's Most Valuable Player.

The Yanks 1955 World Series opponents, the Dodgers, were a team of resolve. Behind Johnny Podres's shutout pitching in the seventh game of the World Series, Brooklyn wrested the world championship from the Yankees. Finally, after five recent Series failures (1941, 1947, 1949, 1952, and 1953), there was no cry in Brooklyn of "Wait till next year!" Mantle saw limited Series action (10 at-bats, one single, one homer) because of a torn thigh muscle and was hobbled when he did play. Said Stengel, pointing to Mantle's legs in the clubhouse after the game 7 defeat, "They were the difference."

Mantle had enjoyed a fine season, but some people still said that he was playing below his potential. These complaints continued to tarnish some of the glow from his performance. So did a comparison that was captivating New York City baseball fans. New York in the mid-1950s was exceptionally well stocked with outstanding centerfielders. The Brooklyn Dodgers had Duke Snider, the New York Giants had Willie Mays, and the Yankee fans had Mantle. People all over the city argued over which centerfielder was the best.

With the 1955 Series two weeks behind him,

a less-than-eager Mantle set off for Japan with his teammates on a goodwill tour that included 24 exhibition games and endless partying. It got so bad one night that Stengel was forced from his slumber chamber to plead for a little quiet. Clad in his red pajamas, the Yankee manager was addressed as "Santa" by one of his charges.

Mantle had always enjoyed partying, but he was a homebody, too. What he really wanted then was to be back in Oklahoma with Merlyn, who was pregnant. So he arranged for a phony telegram that claimed Merlyn was about to give birth and on that basis was able to go from Osaka to Oklahoma. When the baby—the Mantles' second son—was born a couple of months later, the Yankees fined Mickey for leaving Japan under false pretenses.

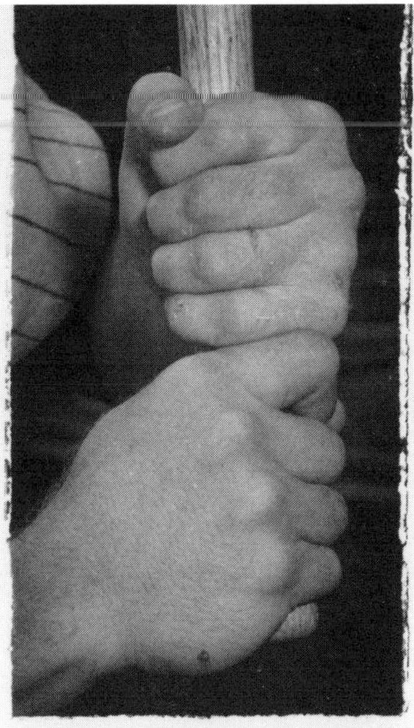
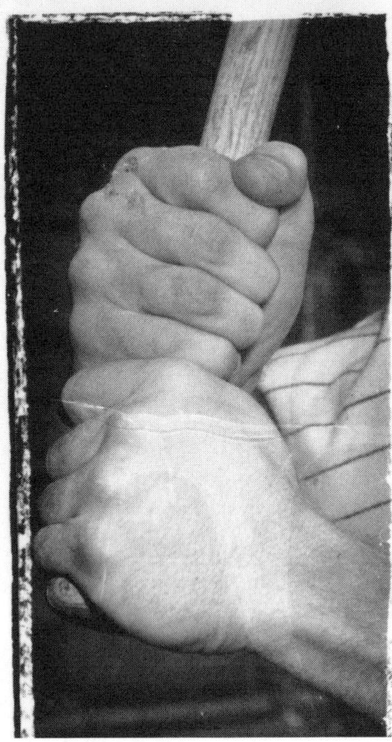

4
THE KID LOOKS DIFFERENT

At the age of 24, Mickey Mantle was still maturing physically and emotionally. He had led the American League in home runs in 1955, but even more was expected of him in 1956. During spring training that year, he constantly drew the eyes of the other players, the sportswriters, and the fans, who were all looking at a bud that was about to bloom.

Mantle had developed into a thick-trunked 195-pound powerhouse. At the same time, he was gaining a newfound self-confidence and shedding some of his shyness. He was in better control of a temper that formerly had him kicking water coolers after striking out rather than sitting down and studying the pitcher. He was, above all else, bringing a cool patience into the batter's box. Pitches outside the strike zone that used to tempt him were less trouble-

Mantle was the most powerful switch-hitter in baseball history. Of his 536 career home runs, 372 were hit left-handed. Ten times in his career he hit both left-handed and right-handed home runs in a game.

some now. He was prepared to wait for *his* pitch.

No one went so far as to suggest that he would one day turn out to be Babe Ruth, Lou Gehrig, and Joe DiMaggio rolled into one, but there was lots of talk about a possible Triple Crown for Mantle. To win "the crown" a player must lead his league in batting average, home runs, and RBIs, a difficult feat.

Ted Williams, who had been both a Triple Crown winner and a .400 hitter, said he saw "no reason why Mantle can't be a .340 hitter this year and hit 40 home runs." Stan Musial, a three-time National League MVP, was even more enthusiastic: "The kid looks different this year. If he hits 60 homers and bats .400, I can't say I'll be surprised." Musial, an outfielder, was still reeling from a Mantle homer at Al Lang Field during spring training. "No home run ever cleared my head by so much as long as I can remember," he said.

Although they seemed willing to concede a "double crown" to Mantle, the one category neither Williams nor Musial mentioned was RBIs. Despite hitting the cover off the ball in 1955, Mantle had accounted for just 99 RBIs. For all their wealth of talent, the Yankees in the Mantle era never had a top-flight leadoff man. That fact, and the many bases on balls served to Mantle, seriously cut into his run production.

Mickey fueled the speculation about his potential with his Opening Day performance in Washington. He made two great running catches and hit a pair of 500-foot homers over the 31-foot-high wall in Griffith Stadium's center field. Behind that wall stood a large tree. According to Stengel, if one of those homers had not hit the tree, "it might be traveling yet." Then he added,

Mantle seemingly won all the awards in 1956. Along with the league's MVP and The Sporting News *Player of the Year awards, he was given the Babe Ruth Sultan of Swat Award in Baltimore. Mantle tries on the over-sized diamond and emerald-studded crown.*

"They tell me that the only other fella which hit that tree was Ruth."

Mantle continued to pound the ball through April and May. With Yogi Berra batting cleanup behind him at an almost equally torrid pace, Mickey was getting a lot of good pitches to hit. Opposing pitchers were not anxious to set the table for the hot-hitting Berra.

Batting left-handed in the first of two Memorial Day games against Washington, Mantle just missed being the only man ever to hit a home run completely out of Yankee Stadium. The majestically lofted ball gave witnesses plenty of time to contemplate the "Is-it-or-isn't-it?" question before the ball hit the green facade that hung from the roof of old Yankee Stadium. It failed to go over by a mere foot and a half.

Mantle hit another tape measure homer in the second game and finished the day leading the league in batting (.425), home runs (20), and RBIs (50). Thanks largely to his output, the Yankees were comfortably ahead in the standings. Mickey Mantle was the talk of baseball—the talk of the country, for that matter.

He had stopped trying to live up to DiMaggio and was simply trying to do the best job Mickey Mantle could do. "DiMaggio," he said, "was the man who could do everything right. There wasn't a thing he couldn't do. I still throw to the wrong base a lot and I drop fly balls."

Mantle was being a bit too modest. For one thing, his speed made it possible for him to reach alley screamers in the "green ocean" known as center field at old Yankee Stadium (the wall was more than 460 feet from home plate), and he had a strong and accurate throwing arm. He was a balanced ballplayer, excelling in every aspect of the game.

His hot hitting continued all season, and he wound up leading the league in batting (.353),

The scoreboard tells the story in game 3 of the 1956 World Series, as Don Larsen throws the last pitch of his perfect game. At bat, Mantle hit a home run, and in the field he used every bit of his great speed to haul down Gil Hodges's 450-foot drive in the 5th inning to preserve the only no hitter in Series history.

home runs (52), and RBIs (130)—the Triple Crown. And for helping power the Yanks to another pennant, he topped it off with the Most Valuable Player Award. Mantle fans in New York now had extra ammunition to use against those who favored Willie Mays and Duke Snider.

Once again, the National League pennant went to the Brooklyn Dodgers, who were determined to defend their world championship. Down 3 games to 2, the Dodgers won game 6 behind Clem Labine, who beat Bob Turley in a 10-inning, 1–0 struggle at Ebbets Field. But the Yankees came back in the all-important seventh game to pummel Brooklyn, 9–0. It was New York's seventeenth world championship.

Mantle collected 3 home runs during the Series, but his greatest moment came not at bat but in the field—at least Yankee pitcher Don Larsen thought so. In game 5, Larsen retired 27 Dodgers in a row for the only perfect game in World Series history. His feat was threatened in the fifth inning, however, when Gil Hodges sent a sizzling drive into Yankee Stadium's left-center field. The ball appeared headed for the wall and extra bases until Mantle came running with everything he had to make a memorable back-handed grab just in the nick of time. As the crowd of 64,000-plus cheered wildly, Larsen breathed a great sigh of relief.

YORK

5

WINNING OVER THE FANS

Mantle still had not reached his prime years—his late twenties and early thirties. His Triple Crown came before he was even 25. So it was entirely understandable that even greater things would be expected from him in 1957.

Mantle came through with a career-high .365 average, and although Ted Williams beat him out for the batting title that year, neither Williams nor anyone else could deny Mantle the MVP Award, his second in a row. His .515 on-base average was the ninth highest in major league history and the chief factor in his again leading the league in runs scored.

Mantle always had a high on-base percentage. Pitchers had to take care not to give him anything too fat, yet he was disciplined enough to lay off the bad pitches. His high strikeout totals had more to do with the viciousness of his swing than any tendency to swing at unhittable pitches. And he drew a bundle of walks (he led the league five times in this category), to go with the many "leg hits" his speed made possible.

Mantle and Willie Mays. In the 1950s, New York fans had a long-running argument as to which center fielder— the Yankees' Mantle, the Giants' Mays, or the Dodgers' Duke Snider— was the best. All three are now in the Hall of Fame.

The hard-hitting slugger could bunt his way on base, too. Mantle was one of baseball's greatest drag-bunters from the left-handed side of the batter's box. With his power forcing the second baseman to play deep, Mantle needed only to push a bunt past the pitcher for an almost sure hit. He was so confident of his ability that he would even drag-bunt with two strikes on him.

His 1957 season was superb, but it could have been even better. For Mickey Mantle came close to achieving the unthinkable—winning a second Triple Crown in a row. As late as August 13th he was perched atop the league in home runs and RBIs, and at .384 he was only 4 points behind Williams in the race for the batting title.

Mantle's 1951 Bowman card.

One of the very things that had gotten him that far, his competitiveness, did him in, however. While playing a losing game of golf, he swung his club at a tree limb in a fit of frustration. Unfortunately, he missed his target and the club did not stop until it had dug into his left shin. The injury—described in the press as "shin splints"—hounded him for the rest of the season. He ended up falling back in each of the Triple Crown categories.

Mantle had another strong year in 1958, leading the league in home runs (42), runs scored (127), and walks (129) as the Yankees won yet another A.L. pennant.

The 1959 season, however, was a bust for Mantle personally and the Yankees as a team. Mantle's batting average skidded to .285, and his league leadership was confined to a single category: strikeouts. It was only the second time in 11 years that New York failed to win a pennant.

Some people believed that no matter what

Mantle used his speed to compensate for lapses in his fielding technique, but because of his fear of injuring his legs, he would rarely dive for a ball. Here he tries to rob Chicago's Eddie Robinson of a home run at Yankee Stadium.

Mantle accomplished, he had the potential to accomplish even more. Although this did not take into account how often serious injuries had hampered his natural abilities, it was true that Mantle did not always push himself as hard as he could.

Mantle greatly enjoyed the social aspects of the game and seemed determined not to miss out on the good times so easily available to a star ballplayer.

Taking into account that Mantle's father and two of his uncles had died young, former teammate Jerry Coleman once speculated: "I just bet that Mantle doesn't think he'll last until he's 50. I was the Yankees' player representative and I know that whenever pensions were brought up, Mickey would always say, 'Well, you don't have to worry about a pension for me. I won't be around to collect it.' He said it kind of kidding, but he meant it, I think."

Although his teammates and even his rivals recognized him as both a decent man and talented ballplayer, many fans resented Mantle's success. Some claimed he was not the gentleman DiMaggio had been. Others wanted him to be more of a showman, like the immortal Babe Ruth. Some critics wondered why Mantle never served in the army, especially during the Korean War. They found it hard to believe that while Mantle was often healthy enough to play superstar baseball, the army had twice rejected him from military service. On two occasions, draft board doctors had refused to enlist him because of his bone disease, osteomyelitis.

All told, Mantle had a serious public relations problem. If the fans booed him in his great years, and they did, they would surely boo him in an off-year like 1959. And they did.

The booing of Mickey Mantle became a Yankee Stadium hallmark. He was even attacked after a game in 1960, an event in which he absorbed a punch to the jaw that put him on a liquid diet for several days.

The low point of his 1960 season, and perhaps of his career, occurred in an August game at Yankee Stadium. Mantle, who was in the midst of a batting slump, came to the plate with one out and new teammate Roger Maris on first base. Mantle was anxious to get a hit but bounced to third. Thinking there were two outs, he loafed to first base. Meanwhile, Maris was attempting to prevent a double play—an attempt in which he was injured while making a hard slide at second base. The fans sent a cascade of boos toward Mantle as Stengel sent him to the bench.

For the next day's game with Baltimore, a disgraced Mantle took his center-field position and was roundly jeered. But in the fourth inning he hit a two-run homer that tied the game, and the jeers turned to cheers. Mantle, in a rare gesture for the shy slugger, tipped his cap to the crowd. Then, in the eighth, he hit another two-run homer to put the Yankees up for good, 4–3. The Yankees moved into first place that day, and Mantle moved into the fans' good graces. Forever, as it turned out.

He finished the season with a league-leading 40 homers, one more than Maris. His own grit

Mantle, who hit .400 in the 1960 World Series, drives in one of his 11 RBIs to help the Yankees win game 3. The Yankees clouted 10 home runs, outscored the Pirates 55 runs to 27, and shattered a 50-year-old record by hitting for a team average of .338. Remarkably, they lost the Series.

Mickey and Casey Stengel, Mantle's manager for his first 10 years. Stengel, who was fired in 1960, said, "They told me my services were no longer desired because they wanted to put in a youth program as an advance way of keeping the club going. I'll never make the mistake of being 70 years old again."

and a sympathetic press that presented a fresh view of the hard-trying Mantle turned off the constant booing. All the fans seemed suddenly to realize how much he really did give of himself, and they elected to show him support in return. Virtually overnight, their hostility turned to adulation.

Maris, who had been obtained from the Kansas City A's before the season began, teamed up with Mantle to form the best power duo since Ruth and Gehrig. Dubbed the "M & M Boys," the pair powered New York to the 1960 pennant. It was Mantle's eighth in his ten years as a Yankee.

The Yankees fought the Pittsburgh Pirates down to the wire in the World Series but were undone by Bill Mazeroski's dramatic ninth-inning home run in the seventh game. Mantle may have played his greatest Series in that battle—a .400 average, 3 homers, and 11 RBIs—and he took the loss hard. Then, the next thing he knew, his only manager in the majors, Casey Stengel, a father figure to him, was fired. Mantle had always regarded Stengel with admiration and affection. It was an unhappy ending to an otherwise satisfying season.

6 THE INCREDIBLE HOME-RUN DERBY

Despite his unhappiness at the end of the 1960 season, Mantle reported to spring camp with a positive attitude in 1961. He liked playing for the new manager, Ralph Houk, who never missed an opportunity to praise him. There was a general feeling in the air, just like the one in 1956, that Mantle was headed for a big year.

The 1961 Yankees, one of the greatest teams of all time, included not just one challenger to Babe Ruth's single-season home-run record but two. Both Mantle and Maris chased after the most famous number in baseball—60, the Babe's home-run total in 1927.

In 1961, the M & M Boys provided a drama within a drama, a home-run derby embedded in a hot pennant race. Even though the 1961 Yanks

The M & M Boys, Mantle and Maris. "I couldn't do any wrong," said Mantle, "after Roger beat me in the home-run race in 1961. Everywhere I went I got standing ovations. All I had to do was walk on the field. It's a lot better than having them boo you."

were an exceptional team (they wound up winning 109 games), they were pressed by a Detroit club unwilling to let go of its own pennant hopes.

Maris, a left-handed power hitter whose stroke was tailor-made for Yankee Stadium and its short right-field porch, was coming off a 1960 campaign in which he hit 39 homers, drove in a league-leading 112 runs, and won the Most Valuable Player Award. An excellent rightfielder who threw well, Maris had only one flaw: he did not hit for a high average. As a newcomer, Maris inherited the "boo birds" who had formerly flocked around Mantle.

It took a while for the home-run derby with Maris to get into high gear. Mantle was the first to go deep, homering in a win over the A's before only 1,947 at a cold Yankee Stadium on April 17th. Maris did not reach the seats until April 26th, the day Mantle homered from each side of the plate to bring his total to seven. But then Maris began to get hot. On Memorial Day in Boston, each homered twice. Now Mantle had 13 homers and Maris 11.

Maris really turned torrid in June, hitting another 15 home runs. But Mantle hung in, and on July 18th, he pulled even with Maris. At that point, both M & M Boys had 35 home runs and were 17 games ahead of Ruth's 1927 pace. A three-homer doubleheader on August 6th moved Mantle into the lead, 43–41.

By this time, the entire nation was following the slugfest, and it seemed that everyone was rooting for one of the players—Mantle, Maris, or Babe Ruth, the sentimental favorite—to emerge with the record.

A spurt of August homers put Maris back in the lead. On the morning of September 3rd, as the Yankees and Tigers headed for Yankee Stadium to conclude the season's most important series, Maris was ahead, 53 to 48. Playing with a pulled muscle in his left forearm, Mantle could hardly swing the bat, but he somehow drove a first-inning pitch over the fence. In the fifth inning, he made a great running catch, and in the ninth, with the Tigers leading, 5–4, he tied the game by pulling home run number 50 deep into the right center-field bleachers. Some 55,000 fans stood up and roared, then watched merrily as the Yankees went on to win.

The Tigers, who had also dropped the first two games of the series, left town $4\frac{1}{2}$ games behind the first-place Yankees. The Tigers were whipped. But, so it turned out, was Mantle.

He awoke the next day, Labor Day, with his arm hurting so badly he had to miss the holiday doubleheader. His legs were hurting, too. Nev-

The 1961 Yankees set an American League record by having six players hit 20 or more home runs. The six were (left to right): Roger Maris (61), Yogi Berra (22), Mickey Mantle (54), Elston Howard (21), Bill Skowron (28), and John Blanchard (21). As a team, they knocked out a record 240 home runs.

Mantle grimaces in pain after drilling his only 1961 World Series hit, in the 4th inning of game 4. After reaching first base, he was removed for a pinch-runner.

ertheless, over the next week he managed to hit 3 home runs to stay within 3 of Maris's 56. He got number 54 in Boston on September 23rd, even though he was very weak and suffering from a bad cold. But then he reacted badly to an injection for the cold and landed in the hospital. An abscess that formed in the injection area had to be surgically drained. Mantle was out of the race for good. The M & M Boys never let the competition get in the way of their friendship. And they never let friendship get in the way of competition, so all Mantle could do now was watch Maris on television and root for his teammate.

Alone in the spotlight, Maris finally tied Ruth's record. And on the very last day of the season, at Yankee Stadium, he blasted number 61 to establish a new single-season mark.

Mantle's 54 home runs were the most ever by

a runner-up and the most ever by a switch-hitter. His home-run ratio of 10.5 homers per 100 official at-bats was bettered by only one man in the history of the game—the Babe himself.

The fans now resented Maris as much as they had once resented Mantle, whom they treated handsomely.

Manager Houk treated Mantle well, too, saying, "As Mantle goes, so go the Yankees." Those encouraging words gave Mantle more self-confidence, not only as a player but as a team leader.

The 1961 World Series pitted the Yankees against the Cincinnati Reds. Still hampered by his abscessed hip, Mantle missed the first games but played in game 3, wincing painfully with every movement. In the next game at the Reds' old ballpark, Crosley Field, he cracked a sure double off the scoreboard in left-center but could barely limp to first base. Once there, he fought back the excruciating pain as sweat poured off his face and blood from his hip oozed through his uniform and ran down his leg. Houk sent in a runner, and that was the end of Mantle's World Series.

While Mantle's teammates admired his courage and appreciated his team spirit, they did not really need him in this Series. It took them just five games to roll over the Reds.

Mantle then went home to Dallas, where he had moved to be closer to his business interests. Mickey was 30 years old, and it was time for a father to be with his kids. He and Merlyn now had four young sons.

7

"THE BEST THING"

St. Louis Cardinals shortstop Dick Groat almost nabs Mickey at second base in the 1964 World Series. In this, Mantle's last World Series, he set lifetime Series records for homers (18), RBI's (40), runs (42), extra-base hits (26), and most total bases (123).

The M & M Boys in 1962 could not match their home-run output of 1961, but they continued to belt the baseball. Maris hit 33 homers and knocked in 100 runs, while Mantle hit 30 home runs, batted .321, and earned a Gold Glove for his excellent defense.

Mantle was playing top-rung ball under a manager who could not have handled him better. He had the love of the fans, and the Yankees were once again on top of the pack, A.L. pennant winners and world champions.

But it was not the smoothest of seasons for Mantle. With the Yankees down to their last out and facing defeat in a game on May 18th, Mantle collapsed in a heap on the first-base line while straining to beat out a grounder. He lay there, writhing in pain from a severely torn thigh muscle in his right leg and an injury to his left knee.

Although Mantle was never 100 percent physically able throughout the season, he captured the Most Valuable Player Award for the third time. He missed nearly 40 games due to injury, but he won the award because of the difference he made: New York had a 75–42 record when Mantle was in the starting lineup and a 21–24 record when he was not.

The following season, 1963, began slowly for Mantle, but in May his bat turned red hot. He beat the A's on May 22nd with an 11th-inning homer that he called "the hardest ball I ever hit." Batting left-handed against Bill Fischer, Mantle timed a fastball so perfectly that the bat bent in his hands on impact. The ball shot toward Yankee Stadium's right-field grandstand and would have cleared the roof had it not been hit in so straight a line. It was still rising as it banged into the old stadium's facade, a few feet below the roof. A physicist later figured out that unimpeded the ball would have traveled at least 620 feet.

The baseball world was still buzzing about this drive when Mantle put a hole in his season that was even bigger than the gap in his 1962 season. His encounter with the chain-link fence in Baltimore on June 5th caused not only pain and further damage to an already banged-up body but forced him to miss 61 games.

He would once again bounce back, heroically, but his injuries were taking a heavy toll. It was remarkable that he could get as much mileage as he did from his battered body. All told he would have operations on both knees, his right hip, and his right shoulder. He broke his foot and several fingers, and he suffered at least six painfully pulled hamstring muscles as well as muscle tears in his thighs and groin.

The injuries not only dictated when he played but interfered with how he played. "Why, if that guy was healthy, he'd hit 80 home runs," Boston's great Carl Yastrzemski commented.

Mantle was aging and so, apparently, were the Yankees, who lost the 1963 World Series to the Los Angeles Dodgers in the minimum four games.

The team managed to make one last great effort in 1964 as Mantle led them to the American League pennant, batting .303 with 35 homers and 111 RBIs. But the Yankees again failed to take the Series. This time they went to seven games before bowing to the St. Louis Cardinals and their star pitcher, Bob Gibson.

The Yankees failure to win their 21st world championship—it would have been Mantle's eighth—was not the fault of their centerfielder. His 3 home runs, one of which won a game in the ninth inning, was tops for both clubs, and he led

By 1967, Mickey's leg injuries forced him to move from the outfield to first base, a position that did not require him to run as much. Here he puts the tag on Detroit's Al Kaline, another future Hall of Famer.

in runs (8) and RBIs (8) as well. With that performance, he established a number of lifetime World Series records: most home runs (18), most RBIs (40), most runs (42), most walks (43), most extra-base hits (26), and most total bases (123).

While no one blamed Mantle for the loss, the same could not be said about Yogi Berra, who had managed the club that year, with Houk moving to the front office as general manager. Before the 1965 season began, Berra, a well-liked Yankee, was fired. Houk replaced him with Johnny Keane, the ex-Cardinal manager.

The Yankees under Keane crashed, and crashed badly, finishing the 1965 season in sixth place. The team was a mix of injured players, aging stars, and potential stars who did not pan out. Clearly, Keane could not be held solely responsible for the team's collapse.

Still, Keane made the mistake of not knowing his personnel. For example, he had Mantle playing in both ends of an early-season doubleheader, and for the following week Mickey could do little more than occasionally trudge to the plate to pinch-hit. As Berra had known, Mantle required periodic resting, and that meant playing him for no more than nine innings a day.

Not surprisingly, Mantle had a poor 1965, playing in only 122 games compared to 143 the previous season. This time he batted only .255 and his home-run output of 19 was little more than half his 1964 total.

Mantle reported to the Yankees for the 1966 season unable to throw a ball as hard as the average Little Leaguer. He had done further damage to his right shoulder (first injured in the 1957 World Series) the previous fall, while playing touch football with his sons. An operation for the

Mickey and Merlyn Mantle, along with their four sons (left to right), Danny, Mickey, Bill, and David, relax in their backyard in the mid-1960s.

removal of calcium deposits and bone chips had been necessary, along with a slow recuperation that extended into spring training. But somehow he was ready to play by the opening of the season.

Indeed, 1966 would prove a good year for Mantle. Houk was back as manager, the Yankees having decided only 20 games into the season to let Keane go. Although Mantle was delighted with the move, it did not prevent the Yankees from finishing last in what was then a single division, 10-team American League.

The 34-year-old Mantle hit a respectable .288 and collected 23 home runs over 108 games. Eleven of those home runs came over 14 games, but the streak ended abruptly when he suffered a torn leg muscle. "Why is it," he lamented to reporters gathered around his locker, "this happens every time things are going well?"

Unit District #5 Elementary
Instructional Media Center - 2

Mantle waves to an enthusiastic fan at the "Mickey Mantle Day" ceremonies, during which his number, 7, was retired.

More than a few people wondered why Mantle put himself through such torture. But he was thankful to be able to play baseball at all. Besides, he could not picture himself making a living any other way.

Mickey was starting to reach career milestones. The biggest came on May 14, 1967, when he hit his 500th major league homer, something only five other players had ever done. In 1968, he passed Ted Williams and Jimmie Foxx on the all-time home-run list, running his total to 536, which, at the time, was third behind Babe Ruth and Willie Mays.

Few people expected the ailing—and aging—center fielder to play a new season, but Mantle himself remained mute on the subject until March 1, 1969, when he announced that he was through. His retirement capped 2,401 games played as a Yankee, a club record.

Mickey Mantle Day was held on June 8, 1969, at Yankee Stadium. Mantle's uniform number, 7, would be retired along with him. After tingling to a long ovation from the 60,000-plus fans assembled, Mantle addressed the appreciative crowd. "Playing eighteen years in Yankee Stadium for you folks was the best thing that could ever happen to a ballplayer," he said. Then, with a catch in his voice, he made reference to Lou Gehrig's 1939 farewell speech in Yankee Stadium, saying he had "always wondered how a man who knew he was going to die could have stood here and said he was the luckiest man in the world. Now I know how Lou Gehrig felt." There was a pause, and then the crowd roared.

On August 12, 1974, Mickey Mantle was inducted into the Baseball Hall of Fame in Cooperstown, New York, along with his good friend Whitey Ford. On hand for the occasion was 84-year-old Casey Stengel.

Since Mantle's playing days, his business investments have not always been lucky, but through various promotional, communications, and business activities, he has had a comfortable post-baseball life.

In retirement, he continues to hit the ball for long distances—although now it is a golf ball and not an 85-mile-per-hour curveball. The golf course may not have the roaring crowds, but the play is just as intense. For Mickey Mantle there is no fun like total, all-out competition.

CHRONOLOGY

Oct. 20, 1931	Born Mickey Charles Mantle in Spavinaw, Oklahoma
May 16, 1949	Signs contract with New York Yankees
April 17, 1951	Makes major league debut as Yankee rightfielder
May 1, 1951	Hits first major league homer, a 450-footer, batting left-handed
Oct. 5, 1951	Severely injures right knee when his spikes catch in a drain cover at Yankee Stadium in game 2 of the World Series
Dec. 23, 1951	Marries Merlyn Johnson in Picher, Oklahoma
May 6, 1952	Father, Elvin "Mutt" Mantle, dies at age 40
April 17, 1953	Hits 565-foot home run in Washington
1955	Leads American League with 37 home runs
1956	Wins Triple Crown, leading the American League in home runs (52), RBIs (130), and batting (.353); wins American League Most Valuable Player Award
1957	Hits career high .365; wins a second Most Valuable Player Award
1958	Leads American League with 42 home runs
1960	Leads American League with 40 home runs
1961	Hits 54 home runs
July 4–6, 1962	Homers in four consecutive at-bats
1962	Wins third Most Valuable Player Award
Sept. 17, 1964	Collects his 2,000th hit in the majors
May 14, 1967	Becomes the sixth player to hit 500 career home runs
Sept. 20, 1968	Hits 536th major league home run; at the time, only Babe Ruth and Willie Mays had hit more
March 1, 1969	Announces his retirement
June 8, 1969	Sees uniform No. 7 retired during Mickey Mantle Day celebration at Yankee Stadium
Jan. 16, 1974	Elected to the Baseball Hall of Fame in his first year of eligibility

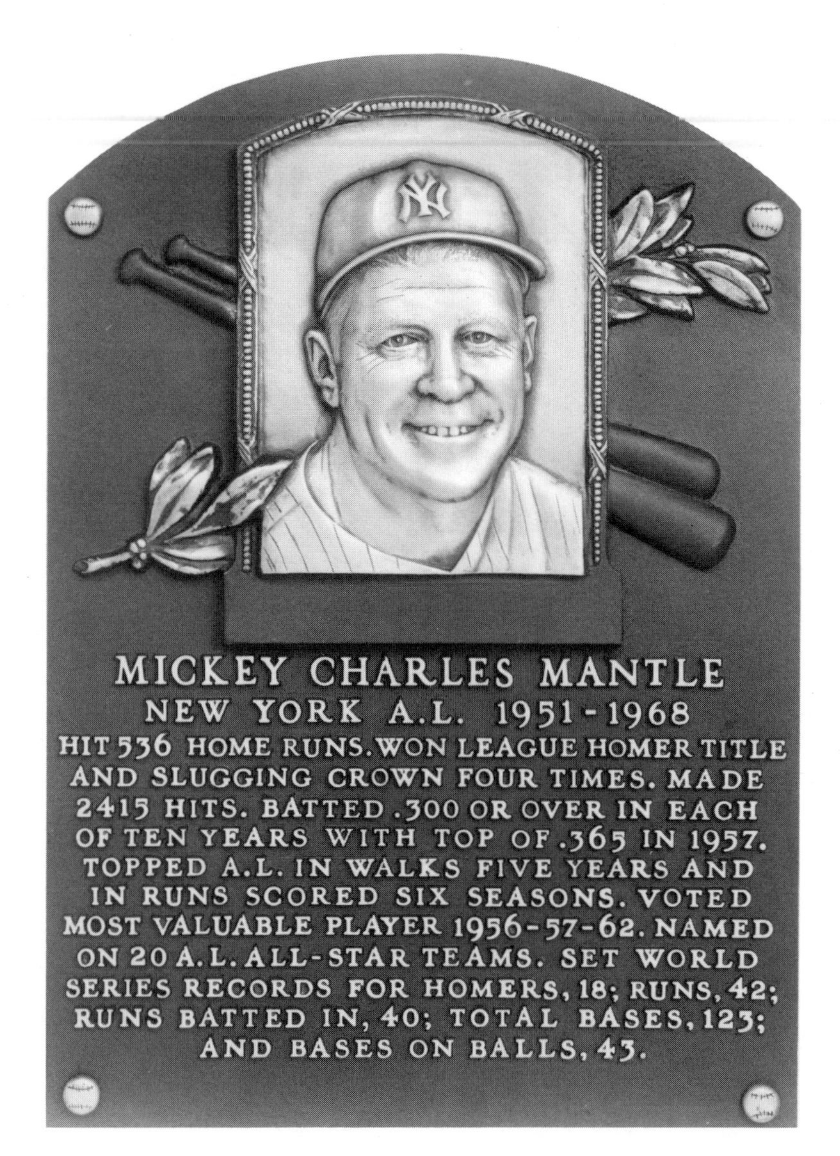

NY
MICKEY CHARLES MANTLE
NEW YORK A.L. 1951-1968
HIT 536 HOME RUNS. WON LEAGUE HOMER TITLE
AND SLUGGING CROWN FOUR TIMES. MADE
2415 HITS. BATTED .300 OR OVER IN EACH
OF TEN YEARS WITH TOP OF .365 IN 1957.
TOPPED A.L. IN WALKS FIVE YEARS AND
IN RUNS SCORED SIX SEASONS. VOTED
MOST VALUABLE PLAYER 1956-57-62. NAMED
ON 20 A.L. ALL-STAR TEAMS. SET WORLD
SERIES RECORDS FOR HOMERS, 18; RUNS, 42;
RUNS BATTED IN, 40; TOTAL BASES, 123;
AND BASES ON BALLS, 43.

MAJOR LEAGUE STATISTICS

NEW YORK YANKEES

YEAR	TEAM	G	AB	R	H	2B	3B	HR	RBI	BA	SB
1951	NY A	96	341	61	91	11	5	13	65	.267	8
1952		142	549	94	171	37	7	23	87	.311	4
1953		127	461	105	136	24	3	21	92	.295	8
1954		146	543	129	163	17	12	27	102	.300	5
1955		147	517	121	158	25	11	37	99	.306	8
1956		150	533	132	188	22	5	52	130	.353	10
1957		144	474	121	173	28	6	34	94	.365	16
1958		150	519	127	158	21	1	42	97	.304	18
1959		144	541	104	154	23	4	31	75	.285	21
1960		153	527	119	145	17	6	40	94	.275	14
1961		153	514	132	163	16	6	54	128	.317	12
1962		123	377	96	121	15	1	30	89	.321	9
1963		65	172	40	54	8	0	15	35	.314	2
1964		143	465	92	141	25	2	35	111	.303	6
1965		122	361	44	92	12	1	19	46	.255	4
1966		108	333	40	96	12	1	23	56	.288	1
1967		144	440	63	108	17	0	22	55	.245	1
1968		144	435	57	103	14	1	18	54	.237	6
Totals		2401	8102	1677	2415	344	72	536	1509	.298	153
World Series (12 yrs)		65	230	42	59	6	2	18	40	.257	3
All-Star Games (13 yrs)		16	43	5	10	0	0	0	2	.233	4

FURTHER READING

Bunning, Jim, Whitey Ford, Mickey Mantle, and Willie Mays. *Grand Slam: The Secrets of Power Baseball.* New York: Viking, 1965.

Devaney, John. *The Baseball Life of Mickey Mantle.* New York: Scholastic, 1969.

Epstein, Ben. *The Mickey Mantle Story.* New York: Henry Holt, 1953.

Ford, Whitey, Mickey Mantle, and Joseph Durso. *Whitey and Mickey: An Autobiography of the Yankee Years.* New York: Viking, 1977.

Gallagher, Mark. *Explosion! Mickey Mantle's Legendary Home Runs.* New York: Arbor House, 1987.

Gallagher, Mark, and Neil Gallagher. *The Yankees.* New York: Gallery Books, 1990.

Golenbock, Peter. *Dynasty: The New York Yankees 1949–1964.* Englewood Cliffs, NJ: Prentice-Hall, 1975.

Honig, Donald. *Mays, Mantle, Snider: A Celebration.* New York: Macmillan, 1987.

Houk, Ralph, and Robert W. Creamer. *Season of Glory: The Amazing Saga of the 1961 New York Yankees.* New York: G.P. Putnam, 1988.

Kubek, Tony, and Terry Pluto. *Sixty-one: The Team, the Record, the Men.* New York: Macmillan, 1987.

Lally, Dick. *Pinstriped Summers: Memories of Yankee Seasons Past.* New York: Arbor House, 1985.

Mantle, Mickey. *The Quality of Courage.* New York: Doubleday, 1964.

Mantle, Mickey. *The Education of a Baseball Player.* New York: Simon and Schuster, 1967.

Mantle, Mickey, with Herb Gluck. *The Mick.* New York: Doubleday, 1985.

Schaap, Dick. *Mickey Mantle: The Indispensable Yankee.* New York: Bartholomew House, 1961.

Schoor, Gene. *Mickey Mantle of the Yankees.* New York: G.P. Putnam, 1958.

Stengel, Casey, with Harry T. Paxton. *Casey at the Bat: The Story of My Life in Baseball.* New York: Random House, 1961.

INDEX

PICTURE CREDIT
AP/Wide World Photos: pp. 33, 53; National Baseball Library: pp. 11, 34, 47, 55, 58, 60; UPI/Bettmann: pp. 2, 8, 12, 14, 17, 20, 22, 25, 27, 30, 36, 39, 41, 42, 44, 48, 50, 56; Copyright The Topps Company, inc.: p. 38

MARK GALLAGHER is the author of *Explosion! Mickey Mantle's Legendary Home Runs*, as well as several books on the New York Yankees. He is a substance-abuse counselor and lives in Germantown, MD.

NEIL GALLAGHER is a graduate of Penn State University and lives in Rockville, MD, where he operates a printing/editorial service company. This is the second book he has co-authored with his son, Mark.

JIM MURRAY, veteran sports columnist of the *Los Angeles Times*, is one of America's most acclaimed writers. He has been named "America's Best Sportswriter" by the National Association of Sportscasters and Sportswriters 14 times, was awarded the Red Smith Award, and was twice winner of the National Headliner Award. In addition, he was awarded the J. G. Taylor Spink Award in 1987 for "meritorious contributions to baseball writing." With this award came his 1988 induction into the National Baseball Hall of Fame in Cooperstown, New York. In 1990, Jim Murray was awarded the Pulitzer Prize for Commentary.

EARL WEAVER is the winningest manager in Baltimore Orioles history by a wide margin. He compiled 1,480 victories in his 17 years at the helm. After managing eight different minor league teams, he was given the chance to lead the Orioles in 1968. Under his leadership the Orioles finished lower than second place in the American League East only four times in 17 years. One of only 12 managers in big league history to have managed in four or more World Series, Earl was named Manager of the Year in 1979. The popular Weaver had his number 4 retired in 1982, joining Brooks Robinson, Frank Robinson, and Jim Palmer, whose numbers were retired previously. Earl Weaver continues his association with the professional baseball scene by writing, broadcasting, and coaching.